ENCOUNTERING
ALIENS

EYEWITNESS ACCOUNTS

by Chris Kincade

illustrated by Cristian Mallea

Consultant:
Jerome Clark
J. Allen Hynek Center for UFO Studies
Chicago, Illinois

CAPSTONE PRESS
a capstone imprint

Graphic Library is published by Capstone Press,
1710 Roe Crest Drive, North Mankato, Minnesota 56003
www.capstonepub.com

Library of Congress Cataloging-in-Publication Data
Kincade, Chris, author.
  Encountering aliens : eyewitness accounts / by Chris Kincade ; illustrated by Cristian Mallea.
      pages cm.–(Graphic library. Eyewitness to the unexplained)
  Summary: "Stories of alien encounters are told using eyewitness accounts in graphic novel
format"–Provided by publisher.
  Audience: 8–14.
  Audience: Grades 4 to 6.
  Includes bibliographical references and index.
  ISBN 978-1-4914-0244-3 (library binding)
  ISBN 978-1-4914-0249-8 (ebook pdf)
1. Human-alien encounters–Juvenile literature. 2. Human-alien encounters–Comic books,
strips, etc. 3. Unidentified flying objects–Sightings and encounters–Juvenile literature.
4. Unidentified flying objects–Sightings and encounters–Comic books, strips, etc. I. Mallea,
Cristian, illustrator. II. Title.
  BF2050.K54 2015
  001.942–dc23   2014007819

Speech and thought bubbles in green are direct quotations from eyewitness accounts.

Photo Credit
Shutterstock: shiva3d, cover (alien face)

Design Elements
Shutterstock: alanadesign, Mika Shysh

        Designer   Production Specialist
       Ted Williams   Laura Manthe

       Art Director   Editor
      Nathan Gassman   Anthony Wacholtz

Printed in the United States of America in Stevens Point, Wisconsin.
032014   008092WZF14

TABLE OF CONTENTS

*Stories in this book are taken from eyewitness
accounts and cannot be proven true or false.

VISITORS FROM OTHER WORLDS

Pilot Kenneth Arnold saw something high above Washington on June 24, 1947, that he couldn't identify. While flying over Mount Rainier, he spotted nine shiny, silver objects zipping across the sky. He said they looked like pie plates that moved "like a saucer would if you skipped it across the water."

THE TRAVIS WALTON ABDUCTION, 1975

A newspaper reporter published Arnold's story about his encounter with the "saucer-like" unidentified flying objects (UFOs). But the reporter paraphrased his words, and the popular term "flying saucer" was born.

THE KELLY-HOPKINSVILLE
ENCOUNTER, 1955

Arnold's mysterious flying saucers weren't the first UFO or alien encounters in history. People have claimed they've seen unexplainable objects in the sky for hundreds of years. But Arnold's encounter sparked new interest in the idea of visitors from other worlds.

THE HILL ABDUCTION, 1961

To this day questions about the existence of aliens remain unanswered. But one thing can't be denied. Hundreds of otherworldly encounters have been reported in the past 60 years. Are these experiences real? Get ready to decide for yourself.

On a rural Kentucky farm, the Sutton family claimed they experienced a terrifying alien encounter.

Their story began when a guest of the family, Billy Ray Taylor, returned from the family well.

You're never going to believe it! I just saw a flying saucer land in the gully, over yonder.

No one believed him.

BARK!
BARK!

At about 8:00 that evening, the Sutton's dog began barking furiously outside. Cecil "Lucky" Sutton, the head of the household, and Billy grabbed their guns.

6

Billy and Lucky fired at the same time. But the creature sprung into a backflip and dashed into the woods.

Once outside, they froze. A glowing green creature walked toward the house. It was less than 4 feet (1.2 meters) tall. It had a large head, round glowing eyes, and clawed hands.

Billy and Lucky then poked their heads outside to see if they'd killed the being. As they stood in the doorway, a clawed hand reached down and grabbed Billy by the hair.

The men made a hasty retreat back into the house. The next thing they knew, another creature appeared at the window. The men fired, blowing a hole in the window screen.

The men fired at the creature on the roof. Then they scrambled back into the house. For the next several hours, glowing creatures continued to peek into the house. Billy and Lucky kept blasting away, putting holes in the windows and walls.

BLAM!

BLAM!

BLAM!

We'll get you yet!

By 11:00 that evening, the Suttons had had enough. They loaded up two cars and drove to Hopkinsville to get the police. When they returned, the police saw many bullet casings and holes in the house, but no signs of the creatures.

You boys sure have made a mess of things around here.

We've been fighting them for nearly four hours.

The police left at about 2:15 in the morning. But the Suttons' night was far from over. The creatures returned. No amount of gunfire could keep them from peering through the windows and holes.

By sunrise the creatures were gone—never to return.

YOU DECIDE

A newspaper report about the Suttons' alien encounter was published the next day. Most people thought the story was a hoax or that the aliens were actually owls. But investigators questioned the seven adults in the Sutton family separately. Their details about the encounter and sketches of the creatures matched up.

CHAPTER TWO

THE FATHER GILL UFO SIGHTINGS
PAPUA NEW GUINEA, JUNE 26, 1959

Father William Gill had just finished dinner at his Anglican mission when a strange sight caught his eye. A bright light in the northwest was approaching the mission. Word of the mysterious light spread quickly. Soon 38 people had gathered to see the extraordinary visitors.

What do you think it is?

I don't know. I've never seen anything like it.

It appears to be some sort of vehicle.

At about 6:45 in the evening, a silent disc-shaped UFO hovered about 400 feet (122 meters) above the mission. Father Gill reported "this blue light—rather like a thin spotlight [shone] skywards to stay on for a second or two, and then switch off."

Most remarkably, four humanlike beings walked around on top of the craft. They ducked in and out of sight as they seemed to work on the ship.

"Look ... it's flying away!"

Father Gill and the other witnesses watched the craft and its riders until about 11:00 in the evening. Then thick clouds and heavy rain set in, and the UFO vanished.

The next night, the UFO visited the mission for a second time. The details of the visit were the same—except one. That night Father Gill and other witnesses waved at the beings working on top of the UFO.

The mysterious visitors waved back.

YOU DECIDE

Father Gill was highly respected in the Australian Anglican Church. While some people were skeptical of his story, investigators found no reason to believe he had lied about the UFO sightings. In fact, 25 other witnesses also gave signed testimonies about what they saw on those nights.

CHAPTER THREE
THE HILL ABDUCTION
RURAL NEW HAMPSHIRE, SEPTEMBER 19, 1961

Betty and Barney Hill experienced one of the most remarkable alien encounters in history. While driving home one night, a bright object in the sky caught their attention.

Do you think that light is coming from a plane, Betty?

I don't know, Barney. Planes don't usually move so randomly.

With his binoculars, Barney could make out the shapes of beings inside the craft. And he realized the pancake-shaped UFO was moving closer.

Barney decided to get a better look while Betty stayed in the car.

It's coming right toward us!

Barney panicked. He ran back to the car and hit the gas. As the Hills sped away, they heard a set of beeping noises. Then they heard more beeps.

Barney, that road sign shows we're 35 miles farther down the road than we were a second ago.

That's impossible!

They also discovered that two hours of their lives had mysteriously vanished.

Two weeks after the sighting ...

Over and over, Betty dreamed about being taken aboard the mysterious craft. Barney also suffered from anxiety he couldn't explain. Eventually, they asked Boston psychiatrist Benjamin Simon for help.

Simon used hypnosis to reach the Hills' buried memories of the UFO encounter. Separately the Hills described very similar accounts.

Through hypnosis the Hills remembered Barney stopping the car after the first set of beeps. Then they were led aboard the UFO. Both were examined by short beings with wide eyes, lipless mouth slits, and hairless heads.

Betty recalled the beings taking hair and skin samples and inserting a needle into her stomach. Barney kept his eyes closed as the beings examined his body with various instruments and studied his false teeth.

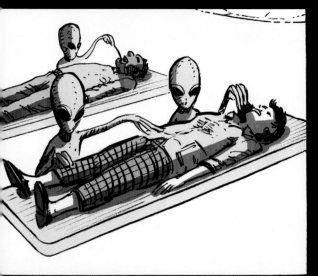

After the exam, the alien leader showed Betty a star map and asked her questions using telepathy. Then he suggested the Hills would forget everything that happened to them that night.

After two hours on the craft, the Hills returned to their car and drove away. Miles down the road, a second set of beeps snapped them out of their dreamlike state.

BEEP! BEEP! BEEP!

Barney, that road sign shows we're 35 miles farther down the road than we were a second ago.

That's impossible!

YOU DECIDE

Dr. Benjamin Simon's analysis of the Hills' hypnosis sessions was unclear. He concluded the Hills did not make up their story. At the same time, he felt their separate hypnosis sessions may have revealed shared hallucinations about a real event. As to what the real event was—he couldn't be sure.

CHAPTER FOUR

ASTRONAUT GORDON COOPER'S UFO

EDWARDS AIR FORCE BASE, CALIFORNIA, LATE 1950S

Astronaut Gordon Cooper's interest in UFOs started before his days in space. One day, while serving at Edwards Air Force Base, he sent two cameramen to shoot photos and film of a new landing system. They returned with pictures of more than just the dry, desert lakebeds.

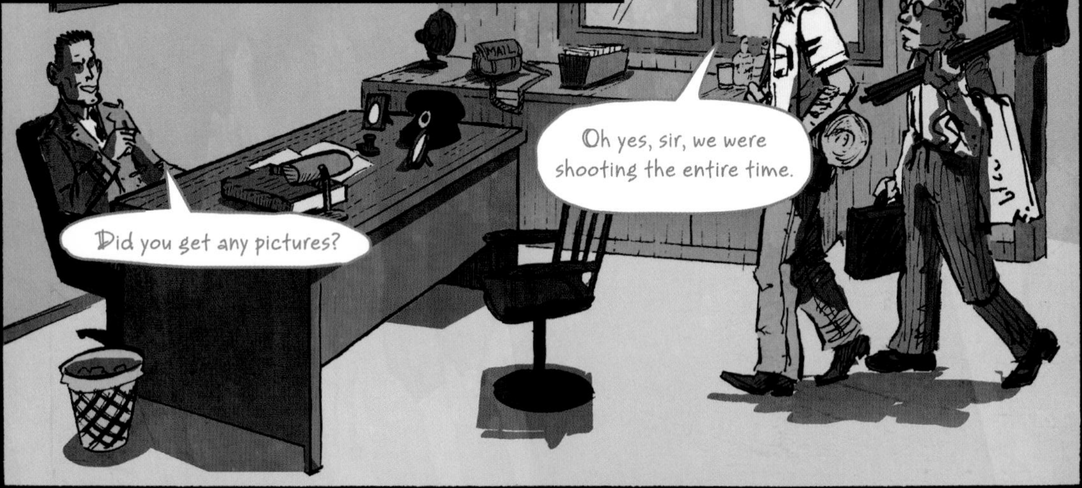
Did you get any pictures?
Oh yes, sir, we were shooting the entire time.

To his surprise, the negatives showed a circular-shaped craft flying above the desert floor.

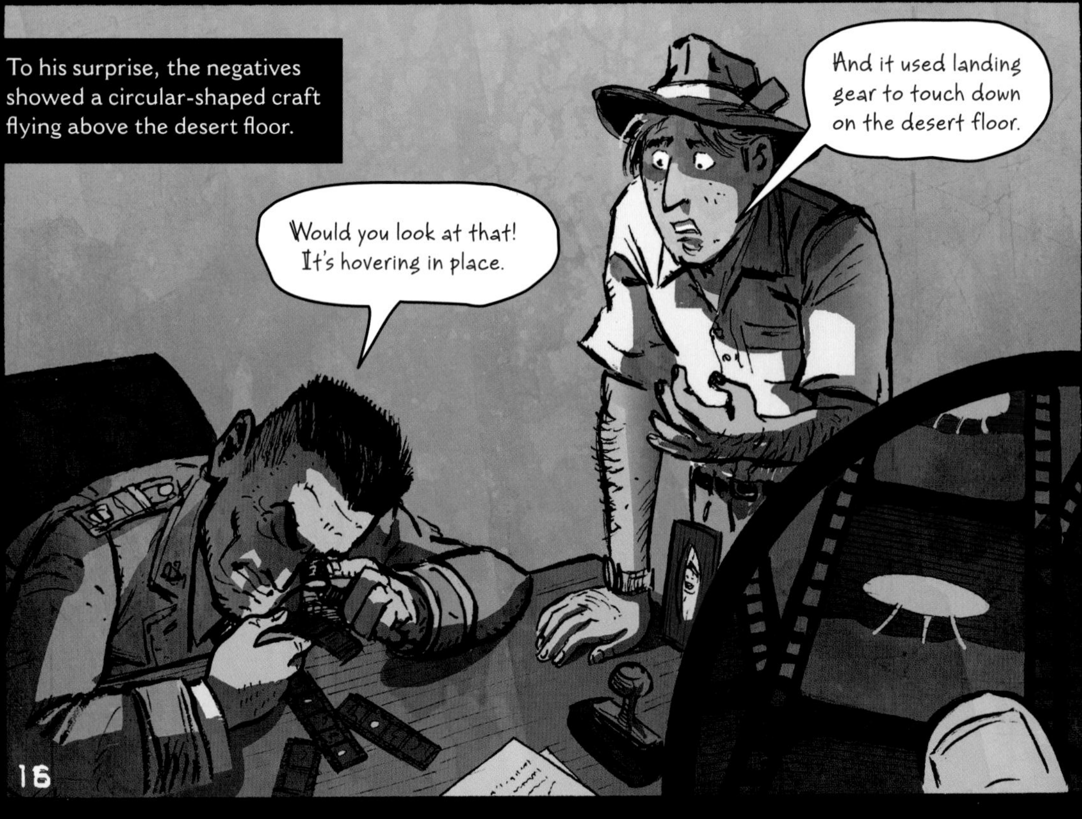
Would you look at that! It's hovering in place.
And it used landing gear to touch down on the desert floor.

After looking at the pictures, Cooper was convinced the object was a UFO.

To Cooper's disappointment, no reply from Washington ever came. In fact, he never saw the photos or film again.

YOU DECIDE

Several newspapers reported the cameramen's UFO sighting. In response, the Air Force released a statement about one month later. They claimed the craft was just a weather balloon. Cooper didn't buy it. He said, "I've never seen a saucer-shaped balloon with three landing gear."

CHAPTER FIVE

THE TRAVIS WALTON ABDUCTION

APACHE-SITGREAVES NATIONAL FOREST, ARIZONA, NOVEMBER 5, 1975

Hey! There's a light coming from that clearing over there!

Few alien encounters are more famous than the case of Travis Walton. Walton and six other woodcutters had spent the day clearing trees near Heber, Arizona. They were heading home when they noticed something unusual.

As the men drove toward the light, they saw a 20-foot- (6-meter-) wide glowing disc hovering above the clearing. Even before the pickup stopped, Walton jumped out for a closer look.

Travis! What are you doing? Get back in the truck!

Gripped by fear, the men watched Walton creep ever closer.

BLEEP! BLEEP! BLEEP!

RUUUMMMBBLEEE!

As Walton got closer, the glowing disc began to wobble.

CRACK!

As Walton crumpled to the ground, the men in the pickup panicked. They sped away, leaving Walton behind.

Walton's fear overtook him, and he stood up to run back to the truck. In that instant, a blue-green beam of light shot from the disc. It launched Walton 10 feet (3 m) into the air.

A few minutes later, they came to their senses and returned to help him. But the hovering disc was gone—and so was Walton.

Five days later Walton's brother-in-law received a surprising phone call.

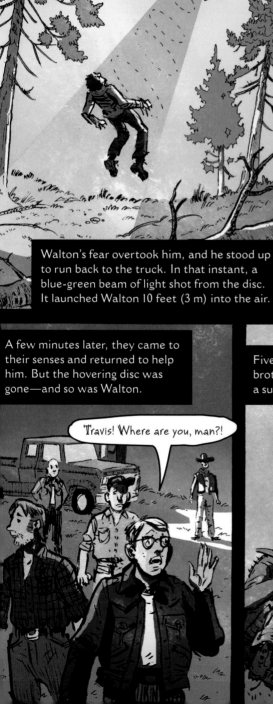

Travis! Where are you, man?!

Hey, Grant, can you pick me up?

Travis?! Is that really you? The police have been searching for you. We thought you were dead!

When Grant picked him up, Walton recounted his tale.

Where have you been, Travis?

The first thing I remember ...

After being struck by the beam of light, Walton recalled waking in a hospital-like room. As his vision cleared, he saw three strange creatures surrounding him. They were short, had domed bald heads, huge brown eyes, and squishy white skin.

Where am I?

Walton staggered off the table and grabbed a tube for a club. He lunged toward the creatures.

Stay away from me! I'm warning you!

When they backed away, Walton rushed from the room.

Walton followed a curving hallway and found a circular room. In the center of the room stood a high-back chair. When Walton approached the chair, the walls of the room became transparent and revealed the starry blackness of space. As Walton marveled at the vision, a tall, blond, humanlike man entered the room.

Then they entered another room where three more human-like creatures stood waiting. They lifted Walton onto a table. He struggled to break free of their grip, but they placed a breathing mask over his face.

... and that's the last thing I remember. Next thing I knew, I was on the side of the highway watching a bright, round light fade into the sky.

YOU DECIDE

During Walton's five-day disappearance, the other men in the truck reported the incident to police. An extensive search for Walton turned up nothing. The men were given lie-detector tests, and the results convinced police the story was not a hoax and did not involve foul play. Later, investigators claimed Walton may have had reasons to fake the abduction, but there was no clear-cut evidence.

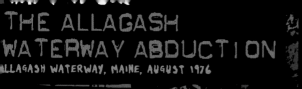

THE ALLAGASH WATERWAY ABDUCTION

ALLAGASH WATERWAY, MAINE, AUGUST 1976

a bright, glowing object in the sky. It moved back and forth as it hovered above the trees. It also changed colors from red to green to whitish yellow. Charlie even tried signaling it with his flashlight.

Jack Weiner, his twin brother Jim, Chuck Rak, and Charlie Foltz were friends from art school. One night on a camping trip, they decided to go night fishing. Before they set out, they built a huge campfire.

Build it bigger! The light will help us find our way back to shore.

What is that?

I don't know, but it must be at least 80 feet around.

Suddenly the object moved toward them. The four friends paddled for their lives, eyes fixed on the campfire burning on shore. In an instant, they were bathed in bright light streaming down from the object.

The next thing they knew, all four were suddenly standing on shore. But something definitely wasn't right.

What just happened?

I don't know, but our campfire should have taken hours to burn down that much.

Unable to understand their experience, the four friends packed up their gear. They returned to their daily lives—but things were far from normal.

As time passed, all four friends began having nightmares. They dreamt about being abducted by creatures with long necks, bald heads, and insectlike hands.

Seeking answers, they turned to a hypnotist for help. In separate sessions, each man shared strikingly similar memories. They all recalled being examined and having samples taken by alien beings.

YOU DECIDE

The hypnotist conducted three-hour hypnosis sessions with each of the four men. He said, "It was the most intense experience I've had as a hypnotist." The fear he heard in the men's voices as they recalled their abduction led him to believe their story. In addition, the men took lie-detector tests after the hypnosis sessions. All four passed the tests. However, one of the four men later stated he was unconvinced that hypnosis could be used to retell past events.

CHAPTER SEVEN
THE PHOENIX LIGHTS
ARIZONA, MARCH 13, 1997

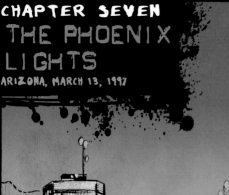

Many UFO sightings take place in remote, rural areas with few witnesses. But every so often, a large city gets an unexpected show. For thousands of people in and around Phoenix, Arizona, one such sighting will never be forgotten.

The first reports came from areas north of Phoenix. At 8:16 in the evening, a former police officer and his family were outside their home near Prescott, Arizona. They reported seeing a cluster of four or five red lights speeding across the sky. The lights formed a V-shaped wedge, similar to a boomerang.

What is that, Daddy?

I don't know son. But I'm calling it into the UFO hotline.

A short time later, witnesses in Dewey, a town just south of Prescott, reported a similar sight. They said the triangular-shaped object slowly glided about 1,000 feet (305 m) above them. As it flew south, it made absolutely no sound.

By about 9:00 that evening, the V-shaped lights flew over the Phoenix area. Thousands of people saw them, but reports of their appearance varied. The number of lights ranged from five to nine. Many witnesses reported the lights looked white instead of red. Even the formation of the lights ranged from sharply triangular to crescent-shaped.

Sightings of the V-shaped lights continued until about 2:00 the next morning. What were these strange lights? No one knows for sure. But for the people who saw them, they will forever be known as the mysterious "Phoenix Lights."

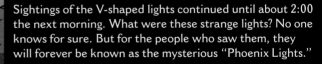

YOU DECIDE

Luke Air Force Base is located about 20 miles (32 kilometers) west of Phoenix. In May 1997 the base claimed flares dropped from one of their aircraft caused the Phoenix Lights. Many UFO investigators don't believe this claim. They say flares could never move together across the sky the way the Phoenix Lights did.

CHAPTER EIGHT

THE ST. CLAIR COUNTY
ILLINOIS UFO SIGHTINGS

LEBANON, ILLINOIS, JANUARY 5, 2000, 4:10 A.M.

When a report of a UFO sighting crackled over his radio, officer Thomas "Ed" Barton looked toward the southeast sky. To his surprise, he saw two bright lights on the horizon. Then, suddenly, the two lights came together as one.

> Be advised, there is a very bright white light east of town. It looks like it's just east of Summerfield, and it keeps changing colors. I'll go over there and see if it looks like an aircraft. It doesn't look like an aircraft, though ... It's not the moon, and it's not a star.

Barton flipped on his siren and raced toward the lights for a better view. He soon realized the object was heading straight toward him—and fast.

> Did I really just see that?

The object approached. When it passed overhead at about 1,000 feet (305 m), Barton could clearly see its triangle shape. Each point of the triangle had a bright white light. Then, in an instant, the UFO turned to the west and streaked away.

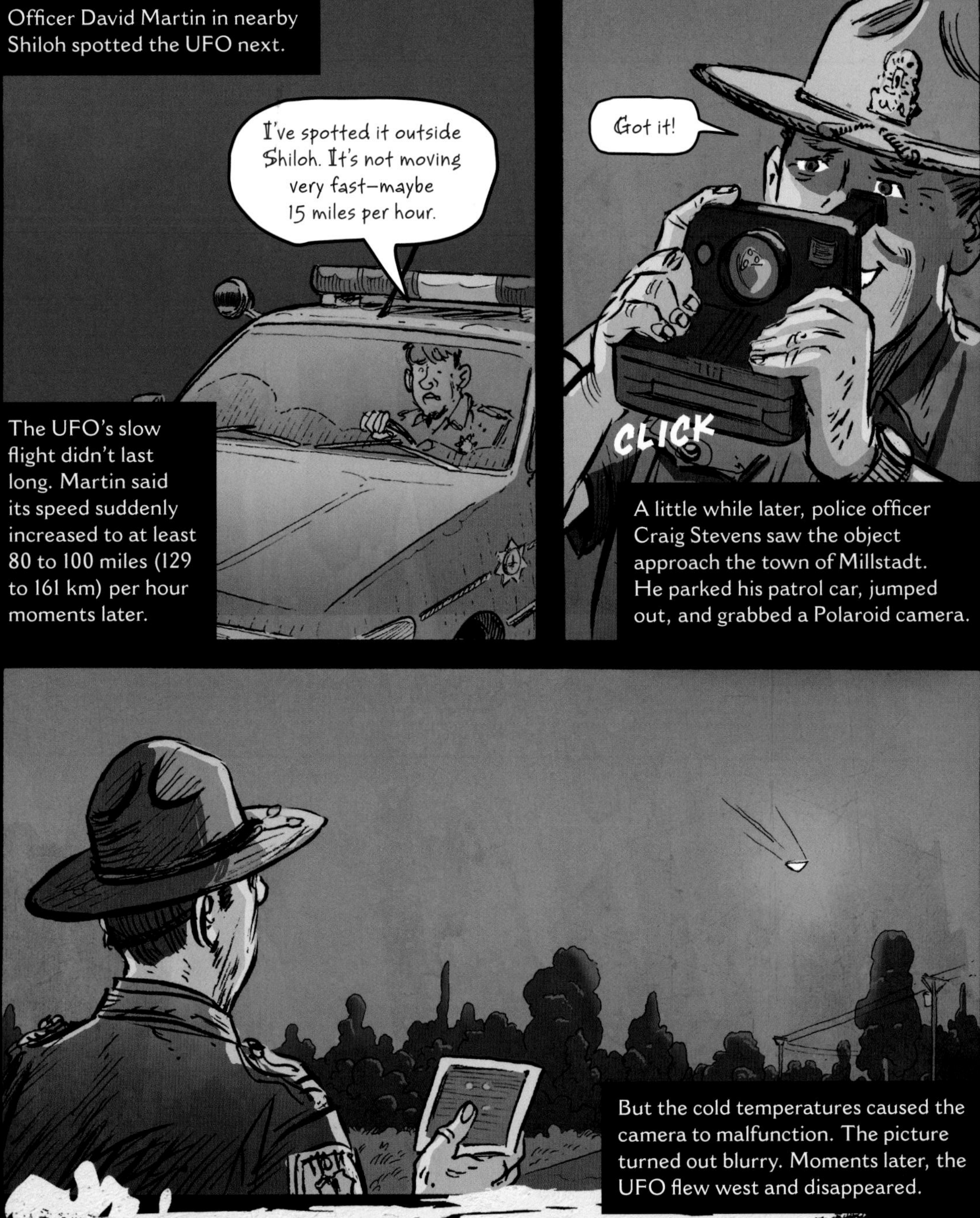
Officer David Martin in nearby Shiloh spotted the UFO next.
I've spotted it outside Shiloh. It's not moving very fast—maybe 15 miles per hour.
The UFO's slow flight didn't last long. Martin said its speed suddenly increased to at least 80 to 100 miles (129 to 161 km) per hour moments later.
Got it!
CLICK
A little while later, police officer Craig Stevens saw the object approach the town of Millstadt. He parked his patrol car, jumped out, and grabbed a Polaroid camera.
But the cold temperatures caused the camera to malfunction. The picture turned out blurry. Moments later, the UFO flew west and disappeared.

YOU DECIDE

Investigators believe the UFO passed within about 2 to 3 miles (3 to 5 km) of nearby Scott Air Force Base. The Air Force stated that no one on the base saw anything unusual in the sky that night. They also said their radar had been turned off during the time of the sightings.

CHAPTER NINE

THE CHICAGO O'HARE SIGHTING

CHICAGO O'HARE AIRPORT, NOVEMBER 7, 2006

As usual, the busy airport bustled with activity. For most United Airlines workers, it was another ordinary day on the job. At least, that is, until they spotted something above the airport that shouldn't have been there.

Hey, did you see a flying disc out by C17?

Sometime between 4:00 and 4:30 in the afternoon, mechanics, pilots, and airline managers began making startling reports.

They had spotted a flying metallic disc above United's Gate C17. Witnesses estimated it was between 22 and 88 feet (7 and 88 m) in diameter. Some said the disc rotated or spun, but others said it didn't spin.

Everyone who saw it agreed on one detail. The UFO hovered in place. It just hung there below the clouds and right above United's gate.

Reports of how long the UFO hovered ranged from 5 to 15 minutes. Then, without even a whisper, it shot straight up.

Hey! It's leaving!

GATE C-17

GATE C-17

The disc flew so fast it punched a perfect circle in the clouds. Through the hole witnesses glimpsed the clear blue sky for the first time that day.

YOU DECIDE

A Federal Aviation Administration (FAA) spokesperson claimed the United workers mistook a "hole-punch cloud" for a UFO. These clouds with perfectly round holes do occur in nature. But weather experts say they only form in below freezing temperatures. The air temperature over the airport that day was more than 20 degrees above freezing.

GLOSSARY

anxiety (ang-ZYE-uh-tee)—a feeling of worry or fear

deny (di-NYE)—to say that something is not true

encounter (en-KOUN-tur)—an unexpected or
difficult meeting

hallucination (huh-loo-suh-NAY-shuhn)—the experience of
hearing or seeing things that are not really there

hoax (HOHKS)—a trick to make people believe something
that is not true

hypnosis (hip-NOH-sis)—a method used to put people in
a sleeplike state in which they answer questions and
easily respond to different suggestions

identify (eye-DEN-tuh-fye)—to tell what something is

mission (MISH-uhn)—a church or other place where
missionaries live and work

psychiatrist (sye-KYE-uh-trist)—a medical doctor who is
trained to treat emotional and mental illness

telepathy (te-LEH-puh-thee)—communication from one
mind to another without speech or signs

testimony (TESS-tuh-moh-nee)—a statement given by
a witness who is under oath in a court of law

transparent (transs-PAIR-uhnt)—easily seen through;
allowing all rays of light to pass through

READ MORE

Burgan, Michael. *Searching for UFOs, Aliens, and Men in Black.* Unexplained Phenomena. Mankato, Minn.: Capstone Press, 2011.

Hile, Lori. *Aliens and UFOs.* Solving Mysteries with Science. Chicago: Raintree, 2014.

Owen, Ruth. *Aliens and Other Visitors.* Not Near Normal: The Paranormal. New York: Bearport Publishing, 2013.

Perish, Patrick. *Are Aliens Real?* Unexplained: What's the Evidence? Mankato, Minn.: Amicus, 2014.

Pipe, Jim. *Aliens.* The Twilight Realm. New York: Gareth Stevens Pub., 2013.

INTERNET SITES

FactHound offers a safe, fun way to find Internet sites related to this book. All sites on FactHound have been researched by our staff.

Here's all you do:

Visit *www.facthound.com*

Type in this code: 9781491402443

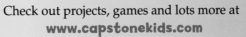

Super-cool stuff!

Check out projects, games and lots more at
www.capstonekids.com

INDEX